HOW TO SELL OVER THE PHONE

ALESSANDRO GENDUSO

TOOLS, TECHNIQUES AND METHODS TO MANAGE A SUCCESSFUL NEGOTIATION PHONE CALL

Summary

INTRODUCTION 3

CHAPTER 1
Positive communication 7

CHAPTER 2
The telephone conversation 10

CHAPTER 3
The use of voice 21

CHAPTER 4
The need 26

CHAPTER 5
The cost-benefit balance 29

CHAPTER 6
Empathy 33

CHAPTER 7
The structured call 41

CHAPTER 8
Rules to make an appointment 61

Acknowledgments 65

Introduction

Why a manual about how to sell over the phone?

Phone sales activity is quite recent. I entered this world in 2001, the year in which many companies were taking their first steps in telephone sales. However, if you look around, there are a large number of publications and pseudo-experts who promise to reveal everything about how to negotiate over the phone, including tricks to *hypnotize* (as they say!) customers on the phone.

Let's face it: how often do we receive commercial calls in the course of the month and how many times are we annoyed?

What should a call be to our benefit, to inform us about the possibility of choosing a product or service on the market often at a better price than listed or published, while staying comfortably at home or in the office, is actually a nightmare for most users.

Because? Simply because it is not a **well done** activity.

In my career, I have listened to dozens of phone vendors, and I have seen several operational training based upon knowledge of the product and upon the main commercial levers to use, rather than how to contact a prospective customer or how to effectively relate to a user in customer base. If we add to this that the objectives are always higher and, for those who work in this sector, low sales often mean risking their job, we understand that the teleselling has been transformed into a wild and mass activity.

A SIMPLE ACTIVITY

The thing that has always amazed me is that in almost all production sectors there is a working method (with procedures to follow) that makes it possible to achieve a very specific goal. These methods are punctually transmitted so that new employees have all the tools to enable themselves to succeed.

In the world of sales, however, very often the success in this profession, more than taught with structured modalities, is left to the free initiative or to the individual characteristics (appeal, charisma of the person), throwing the new employees in the market and allowing the market itself to determine who is better suited to survive without self-elimination due to the failure to achieve the objectives. A Darwinist method that in the past has literally *burned* hundreds of people who now see the world of sales as smoke in the eye or as the only alternative to unemployment.

Rarely, in sales formations, have I observed teaching methods, tools, and practical suggestions on how to deal with the business. Coming into contact with several inside sales departments during my career, I noticed that very often, the initial training to new employees is carried out by providing them with simply basic notions on communication (perhaps plundered from the web or some manual) and then tons of material to study on the commercial offers and on the promotion of the moment.

Even more rare is the possibility given to those who approach this world for the first time, and especially to candidates who have never done sales activity, to understand how to manage, from the beginning to the end, a phone call with the aim to sell something.

This manual will not reveal arcane tricks or bomb techniques that are unknown to most. Simply, it will teach you - or will put you in a condition to teach other people - how to propose something over the phone, whether your purpose is to give information to a customer, to sell them something, or to make an appointment for yourself or for your salesmen in the field.

The defined activity of *telemarketing* in fact comprises of two processes that are managed differently today. One is the *complete* telephone sales, which closes the entire sales cycle, from the first approach to the customer's approval (usually signed up with a verbal order). The other is the activity of making appointments, which is done in a widespread way to support the salesmen of any company who are moving on the national territory everyday.

The two activities, as part of the same family of **telephone activities**, are radically different: they are two similar professions, but at the same time very different from the management of the customer and the telephone call, up to post-call mechanics.

When an employee has to make an appointment for a salesman he just has to arouse curiosity and interest in the product/service. Those who carry out this type of activity can have peculiarities that do not necessarily have to be those of an expert salesman: it is sufficient that they be skilled in dialectic and are able to well explain to the customer the reason for the visit highlighting the basic advantages.

Instead, those who sell a product/service by phone must necessarily be salesmen made and finished, because they have to manage the entire cycle of the sale, and must be prepared on the management of all objections regarding the product or service sold.

Generally, whoever does or has previously done teleselling can easily make appointments activities (with appropriate variations in its communicative techniques, thus avoiding making the mistake of giving *too much information*). On the contrary, those who create appointments will hardly be able to switch without impacts and without training investment towards the activity of teleselling.

According to Bob Davis, founder of Robert C. Davis and Associates, a renowned customer contact consultant, «the first 30 seconds of an outgoing call are critical. There is a need for a statement to show that the call will be of value to the customer, and more importantly during the first 30 seconds, there must be a question that involves the customer on an emotional level and starts a conversation of quality. During the call, the telesales agent must demonstrate a sincere interest in the customer.»

In this text we will also talk about INBOUND and OUTBOUND because they are two activities, even in this case, similar but at the same time different. Making a *cold* call to sell requires a lot more technique and a lot more persuasive skills than receiving a call from which to generate a sale.

This handbook will teach you how to manage and conduct a commercial call to sell a product or service. It does not contain magic formulas or theoretical hypotheses, but tools, notions and concrete methods that are based on practical daily experiences and which are known by the most experienced telephone vendors. These notions, if applied immediately once you have finished reading, will improve your negotiating skills and give you the opportunity to be more effective in selling.

In general, it is my wish is that you be more useful for all your daily sales and customer care activities.

Alessandro Genduso
algendus@gmail.com

Chapter 1

Positive communication

In the film "The negotiator", Samuel L. Jackson plays Danny Roman, the best negotiator in Chicago in kidnapping cases, who finds himself the victim of a conspiracy. Hoping to prove his innocence, Danny decides to enter the headquarters of the Department of Internal Affairs and take the office staff into hostage. So he reverses his role as negotiator in a hostage situation, trying to figure out who's framing him.

During a famous scene from the film, Danny is called by a colleague who wants to convince him to free the hostages, teaches us a great truth that applies as much to the negotiators, as for sellers: you must never say NO!

The **NO** as he says in the film, «eliminates the options.» In our case, responding to a client, «I cannot help it», «I do not have that article», «I have no solutions to give you» does not generate undoubtedly positiveness.

The first thing we learn, then, is that communication should always be positive: we must emphasize effectively the benefits and advantages, use positive and enthusiastic terms to describe our product / service, be fair and transparent in recounting weaknesses and avoid words with a negative connotation that can annoy customers.

It is the concept of so-called *keywords* that can have a positive or negative connotation and, precisely for this reason, should be used wisely. We will discuss in detail in Chapter 2.

Another concept to metabolize and that has an enormous importance in the positive communication, is the way in which the problem is formulated affects how the individual perceives the starting point (or *status quo*), compared to assessing the possible outcomes of their actions. It may seem trivial, but the *how* things are said is as important as their content. Statements and questions in one way rather than another may have totally different effects.

The psychologists Amos Tversky and Daniel Kahneman have demonstrated it through the famous experiment of the "Asian Disease Problem". After selecting two groups of candidates, Tversky and Kahneman submitted a question asking participants what they would do if the choice depended on them.

The problem was this: «Imagine that the U.S. is preparing for the outbreak of an unusual Asian disease, which is expected to kill 600 people. Two alternative programs to combat the disease have been proposed.»

A first group was offered a choice between two *emergency programs*:

- **program A:** 200 people are saved
- **program B:** 1/3 chance of saving everyone, 2/3 chance of not saving anyone

Two other *emergency programs* were offered to the second group:

- **program C:** 400 people die
- **program D:** 1/3 probability that nobody will die, 2/3 probability everybody will die

From a viewpoint of the programs A and B contents are equivalent respectively to the C and D programs: yet the responses of the two groups were profoundly different. In the first group they selected the program A in 72% of cases and the program B in the remaining 28%; in the second group the first choice (78%) fell on the D program while the program C was preferred only in the remaining 22% of cases.

It is apparent that the first group of candidates underwent a message in which prevailed positive elements, while the second group was, however, exposed to negative content. In case of doubt, therefore, the human being tends to choose the positive, even when, as in this case, the success is entrusted to the calculation of probabilities rather than certainties. In the first group, then, the certainty (the solution "A") was chosen massively; in the second test most candidates chose to rely on probability rather than the negative reply.

Adopting positive communication and giving certainty to the customer are two of the axioms on which a good negotiation is based. This argument will also be resumed in the next chapters; In any case it is good to know that the levers are numerous and knowing how to use them makes the difference between the success and the failure of a conversation with aim of achieving a sale.

Chapter 2

The telephone conversation

The secret of a good call is to differentiate it from all those that the customer receives or has previously received. In this business you have to be original. While you are reading this book, many companies are calling customers to offer products or services. To be successful, you have to stand out from the crowd. Making a *standardized* call does not appeal either to the person being called nor generate trust, it just gives a sense of an assembly line and repetition to the customer, who surely will not be impressed. The same repetitiveness will also depress the seller, forced to carry out sterile and monotonous work. In this work you need the utmost creativity, and that is why I personally abhor the conversation scripts (see Chapter 7).

How many times have you been called and found a competent person who can relate correctly to you? I think hardly ever. Often the sellers, in the haste to make the proposal, the hassles of the objectives and the insistence until the exhaustion builds a barrier with the customer that becomes insurmountable. Instead what you have to do as a good seller is to break down the barriers of communication and seek, first of all, to establish a fruitful dialogue with the customer; only then will it be possible to apply the previously studied sales techniques, it is useful to ensure that the other party has purchased the product/service.

First, then, we must establish a proper dialogue with the customer: without this, there cannot be any trade negotiation. You can be the greatest experts of persuasion, but if you do not get to talk to the customer it is clear that everything is in vain. Establish a *cold dialogue* with a client who is called for the first time is not easy. It is flaunting the concept of *empathy* with the customer, often abusing the word in all communication courses and sales, but what does it really mean entering in *empathy* with the customer? How do you do it in practice? We will discuss it in detail inside chapter 6.

Keywords

Communicating on the phone properly when the aim is to sell something, means carefully choosing the words. For this we use the keywords, words that arouse the feeling that we wish to stimulate, possibly positive feelings!

For example, saying to a customer «you will pay a 10€ bill» is not a wise choice. "Bill" is undoubtedly a negative word, which reminds us of the many (and expensive) payments to be made monthly. Say instead «in the next invoice you will find a charge of 10€» or even «you could do a one-time payment of 10€» to make *light* of an annoying concept of paying something.

Words such as tax, bill, obligation, penalty, will always be perceived by the customer as *black* words, words that certainly do not create positive feelings and which may compromise our negotiation. Do you remember when the Italian minister Padoa Schioppa said «taxes are a very beautiful thing» making him very unpopular? Clearly no one tried to analyse the real message he wanted to transmit, namely that taxes are «a civilized way to collectively contribute to essential goods such as education, security, environment and health.»

A famous Italian retail chain, with outlets throughout Italy, recently launched a promotion **3 + 1**; basically if you buy four products, you pay for only three. To determine what the free product is, the claim reads: «By purchasing 4 products you will get the least expensive product for free» But was using the word *expensive* a wise choice? I wouldn't have used that word. Meanwhile, because *expensive* is a word with clear negative value, and then, expressed in this way, the concept attributes the characteristic of *expensive* (= excessive high price, see Chapter 5) to all products chosen. It certainly was not with the intention of marketing that brand, but, in my opinion, the attribution that gives the claim to the products of the brand is not positive.

Words such as *opportunities, advantage, benefit, optimization* are words of positive value which we will use as many times as we want to capture the customer's attention. But do not abuse it: recently the words *promotion* and *offer* that in our mind are synonymous of excellent shopping opportunities have lost their edge, because their use is (and has been) exploited ad nauseum. Now people only buy items *on sale* although maybe it turns out, in retrospect, that the offer is nothing more than the listed price, specially created only to lure the unwary who allow themselves to be manipulated by this magic word.

The retail world (especially the large distribution), has accustomed us to be alert if there are *promotions* to always look at the *offers* on the web or on flyers, do not miss the *discounts* and *sales*, to rush to the store to purchase if *price under cost.* Nowadays the average consumer is hunting for these mythical words, and for this reason it happens more and more often to see in the entire hypermarkets dense walls of products with at the center some shelves totally empty, with a tag above which is written in characters clearly visible **PROMOTION** or **OFFER** in order to indicate the discounted product which, of course, has now been plundered.

But the abuse of this technique has meant that now the customer, accustomed to suspect the existence of commercial tricks behind these words, will be wary and have a cautious attitude. You will notice that the word *free* has recently disappeared from all promotional campaigns a word that has been greatly abused, since it has now taken a counterproductive meaning.

Robert Cialdini, an American psychologist and professor of marketing at Arizona State University and perhaps the greatest expert in the world of persuasion science, in one of his books "Yes!: 50 Secrets From the Science of Persuasion" devotes a chapter to what is given *free*, entitled "when a tribute becomes an outrage".

Cialdini tells us about Dr. Priya Raghubir's study and how this scholar of social sciences has ascertained through tests that when consumers are offered a tribute to induce them to buy a product, the perceived value and the desirability of the homage as an object in itself risk abruptly to decline. The tests of Dr. Raghubir confirmed, in fact, that people perceived a much lower value of the homage if coupled with the product purchased, and instead a higher value (even of 35%) if the object was proposed, alone, for sale.

Why does this happen? Because something *free* for us is something that has no value. If someone gave you a pen, and you happen to forget it somewhere, surely you would not regret the loss that much. But if you had paid even one euro, then perhaps you would have been less distracted, and you would have been more careful not to lose it, since the fact of having lost it would have annoyed you (as well as hurting you financially).

This makes us understand that the word *free* should never be used. If a product or service is also bundled, it must always be specified that one of the two is «included in the package price», always specifying to the customer what is the commercial value of the single product, value that the customer would not have perceived without our specification (thus completely nullifing the importance of the homage).

How to say things

As we have seen in the previous chapter, a similar concept, expressed in different ways, can produce different reactions. Robert Cialdini in the book quoted before, tells us of an episode concerning telephone reservations at the restaurant.

As we know, a restaurant almost always accepts reservations by phone; but it happens that those who reserve do not show up, nor do they even bother to let the restaurant know. If the reservation includes many persons, perhaps on a public holiday when large number of clients are expected, the failure to respect the reservation severely damages the income of the restaurant.

The owner of a restaurant has reduced the percentage of people who do not respect the reservation by simply modifying the sentence to tell the customer who has made a reservation, transforming a statement into a question. The person who took the reservation in the past, in fact, ended the call saying: «Please call us if you want to cancel the reservation.» Now, on the other hand, the customer is asked a question. They are asked: «Would you be kind enough to call if you want to cancel your reservation?», prompting the customer to answer «Yes». Thanks to this simple modification, the percentage of no-shows has decreased from 30% to 10%.

How come? The effect of the psychological mechanisms of our mind, which require us to be coherent with what we say and to be socially acceptable. The *principle of consistency* so called by Cialdini, can also be exploited in other ways, for example during a business conversation with the customer; the questions asked during the interview, in fact, must serve to make us understand the profile of the customer. If so we ask our interlocutor, for example, if they enjoy going to the movies and if he responds yes, we can be sure that the course of the conversation will remain consistent with this statement and will hardly deny having said it nor will he deny his passion for the movies.

The good salesman leverages the information collected, and if he is proposing, for example, tickets for the cinema, a discount card, or a subscription to pay TV, he can clearly cite the answer previously given by the customer and use it to strengthen his negotiation. Downstream your proposal the customer might or might not be interested, but will never deny that he declared that he loves cinema!

The right word to the right person

Sometimes it only takes a couple of words to unlock the indecision of the purchase. How many times do we go to buy something but we are undecided and hesitant whether to buy a certain item? Sometimes it is enough that our companion (wife/husband, friend) tells us a single sentence to convince us definitively that the object is what we need: «It is the green you like», «Yes, but this model does not have it», or «it costs a lot but it is of good quality and will last a long time».

If the accompanying person replaces the (good) seller, here it becomes clear that they use the right arguments applicable to the individual customer that guarantee success in the sale. But how does a seller who has known the customer for a few minutes only to have the same appeal/credibility/knowledge of the accompanying person?

Another important word comes into play here: **personalization**. The future of telephone sales will be based on customizing the tailor-made **sewn** call on the other end of the line. Enough of the massive calls, hundreds of numbers called to get a sale! In the future you will always have to go on customizing the phone call built on the tastes and preferences of the interlocutor. The saying *few but good* does not currently apply to telephone sales will have to become more and more the *leitmotif* in the coming years.

And here comes into play a very important axiom: *selling* is not selling something to someone: on the contrary, it is just an act of communication. It is nothing more than the transmission of the benefits and benefits of a single product/service from the seller who knows them perfectly to his interlocutor (the customer) who does not know them yet. The more the seller improves on this transmission operation, the more effective the sale will be.

But how can I transmit benefits tailored to the customer if I do not know him? How do I build **his** offer? Note that I did not quote casually **his** offer: when you talk to a customer you should always use possessive pronouns. «Your fare», «Your subscription», «Your wine»... The possessive pronoun gives the customer the feeling that for the seller it is as if the product is already in his possession.

Another thing: never use the conditional in the phone conversation. It is a sign of uncertainty, of the possibility that the sale will not go through. «You might receive this set with only...», «You would have a discount of...», «You would save interesting figures...» The conditional should not be used because it denotes a possibility, instead a good salesman must always give a feeling of security when conversing with a customer. An effective seller must always be sure of the quality of their product and the convenience of their proposal, as well as being sure that the product is suitable for the customer with whom you are talking. And since this security must never fail and it must also be stated during the conversation with the client, the seller will take care to always use present tenses or, better yet, the future tense.

We listen to the same sentences with the use of the verb in the future: «You will receive this set with only...», «You shall have a discount of... », «You will save interesting figures...» Don't they sound much better already?

There is a passage of a film that I often show during my training courses: it is "Crimen Perfecto", film of 2004 directed by Álex de la Iglesia. This is comedy in which the main character, an aspiring director, participates in a contest organized by the company where he works, a large retail chain, to become "responsible for the floor". During a tasty skit in which he challenges himself to sales blows with his direct competitor, he is about to lose the challenge when, almost at the end, he manages to convince a customer to buy an expensive fur and win the competition.

In the passage where the protagonist tries to **woo** the customer, there are two jokes particularly significant. To stimulate his curiosity, in fact, the protagonist says with confidence to the customer: «I think you would need different things.» Incredulous the client asks: «Do you think so?» he retorts, decided: «I don't think so. I KNOW.» And to prove again the conviction of his assertion, it represses the customer saying: «I know what it is... and I have it.»

Security must always distinguish the conversation to sell. First of all, without careful preparation it is difficult to sell a product, but especially because, in the eyes of our interlocutor, we always have to position ourselves as *credible* interlocutors. Being *credible* means being competent, having the answers, giving certainty by accompanying what we say with logical evidence. Of course you cannot know everything, and it might happen that you do not know how to answer a customer's question; but in this case, it is much more professional to take the time to inquire in a complete way and then give the right answer, rather than to climb on the mirrors and stutter or give inconsistent answers (and in the most serious cases even wrong), to win the customer! Because in this way you do not build a customer portfolio, but, on the contrary, you destroy the image of your company.

A commercial call

In commercial phone calls, the most common mistake you make, especially for those who are novices, is to fill the silence of communication by continuing to talk. Maybe because you want to express so many concepts all together, or to eliminate that feeling of *emptiness* within the conversation. In any case, it is the most wrong thing that you can do in a commercial phone call. It must be clear that the effective call does not have to be a long monologue in which our interlocutor is struggling to fit in: when, in fact, the client is forced to say «sorry if I interrupt...» it means we're totally wrong about the communicative mode.

In an effective telephone conversation, you have to make frequent pauses and leave ample space for the customer to fit in, ask questions, give feedback. And, if the customer did not (thus remaining silent), we must be the ones to stimulate it through *control questions* (see next paragraph). The conversation must be dotted with sentences followed by pauses, such as the pattern drawn below.

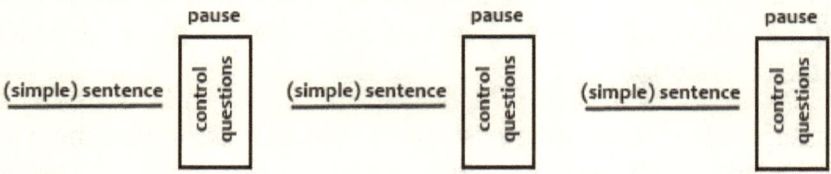

Since the telephone conversation itself is a source of great misunderstanding (also due to *technical* causes: poor reception, disturbed signal, etc.), it must be as schematic as possible. Sentences must be simple – with a subject, a predicate and a complement – and especially short. You cannot make complex or articulated sentences, otherwise you will quickly lose the focus of your interlocutor.

Control questions

When we speak normally, out of 10 words we hear, we listen to 8, we understand 7 and we metabolize 4. This is not because we are stupid, but for a mechanism of cognitive economy put in place by our brains, which must optimize the resources of *memory* and schematize for concepts. So the brain, which cannot remember every single word, stores only the most important words (the famous keyword), which is why they are so important.

As the Palo Alto school taught us, **silence is communication** too. So the silence of the client on the other end of the phone expresses a very precise concept: perhaps the customer has understood everything and is pondering a decision (unlikely) or maybe he has not understood anything and is listening to try to understand their interest (more likely). Maybe he really wants to know more and listens to you with interest, or maybe he is just doing something else while you talk and so he is not even following you.

Imagine talking on the phone with a friend of yours, and hearing only silence at the other side of the wire: I highly doubt that you would continue to talk, but you would interrupt to ask if the person at the other end is listening to you, whether or not the line is failing, or something happened to your friend. This attitude, which applies to everyday life, and must also be applied to calls to sell.

The questions of control are questions that we need to understand if the customer is following us, if they have understood the concepts, but also and above all to get feedback. Questions like «Have I been clear in explaining the modalities? », «What do you think? », «Do you want us to elaborate on some particular points? » or «What makes you perplexed? » are all constructs that allow us not only to understand the direction that the conversation is taking, but also maintaining the rudder while taking high the level of attention of the customer, another key factor that we will discuss in the next paragraph.

The focus curve

The level of attention of our interlocutor is another parameter to be monitored carefully during a telephone conversation. It is very high at the beginning (when there is *curiosity*) but it will tend to collapse drastically after the first few seconds of dialogue. Imagine a Gaussian curve: having understood what we want to talk to them about and satisfy their initial curiosity, the customer will suffer a precipitous drop of his level of attention. It will be our task to raise this level and keep it alive for the duration of the conversation, feeding it continually as we feed a wood when it is going to go off; it is done by continually involving our interlocutor with relevant topics and for him engaging (not keeping it futilely!) until the happy conclusion of the phone call.

As John Medina, molecular biologist of the University of Washington writes in his book "The Brain: Instructions for use", after a few minutes of a meeting or presentation, the brain "pulls the plug". It is a natural trend, but you can fight knowing that the brain better processes the stimuli loaded with emotional content. It keeps them longer in memory and recalls them more accurately than neutral memories. Translated at the commercial level, it means arousing emotion in the customer involving him in the *story* of the product/service. The word *tale* is not used at random because, as Medina says, recounting anecdotes and providing examples improves the coding of the memory because it allows to compare the new information with other data present in the brain, thus facilitating the mental associations.

The theory of the *attention curve* unequivocally shows the inability of the human mind to maintain the same high level of attention over a long period of time. The curve shows that attention can be maintained at high levels for a short period of time (10-15 minutes), then the decay begins that can proceed with a certain speed: as seen from the graph, after the first 5 minutes we have the maximum peak of attention, the attentional erosion operates from 15 minutes, so the maximum attention we can take is for about 10 minutes before the decay.

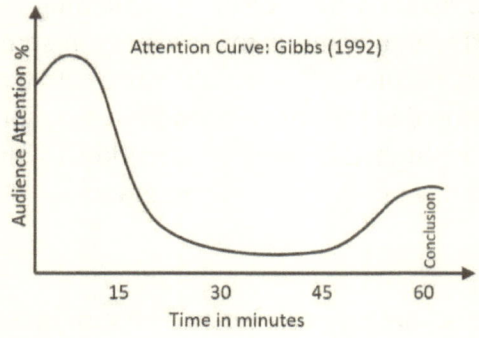

To keep up the level of attention the use of the voice is also very important, which we will talk about in the next chapter.

The energy

One thing that no one says in a training dedicated to telephone sellers, is that those who do this kind of work must learn to ration the daily energy well. Among all the factors that affect the success or failure of a sale, an important part is given by the psychological predisposition that the seller has at the time of the negotiation, contributing various factors (personal or not) among which however stands out in an important way the energy that each individual possesses and uses.

Consider that the telephone sale consists of a few simple parameters:

1) The List of customers to be called (more or less profiled)

2) The Product for sale (more or less appeal)

3) The seller (more or less performing)

The mix of these 3 variable parameters determines the sales volumes.

Within a sales team, since the lists are the same for more people, the product for sale is the same for everyone, the only parameter that we can and must take care of and that we have to treat in a particular way is our ability as sellers.

Going back to talk about energy, imagine a salesman as a pile: He starts his working day full of energy, but as he clashes with the trash, with the answering machines, with customers who waste time unnecessarily or who treat him badly, gradually ending its *charge*. Taking the tiredness, his efficiency decreases drastically, until it reaches the point that, even if he had a customer on line willing to buy, probably would not be able to acquire it.

It is a big mistake to think that the first call of the day and the last will be done in the same way or with the same enthusiasm. That's why, especially in this job, it's essential to optimize your energies. But what does *optimize* mean? It means saving the forces during the calls that we perceive are unproductive and invest instead with those customers who can really bring us value.

Rationalization is always necessary for a question of numbers: if at the beginning of the day you have 100% of energy to spend, and you invest a 5% on each customer, the twentieth customer will not have the right charge to deal with a challenging negotiation. But how do we operate this rationalization? How to understand if the customer with whom we are talking is worth 5% of our energies, 10% or even 20%? What does it mean to invest in the right customers?

For example: If I call a customer who asks me a thousand questions about a product/service but he makes me understand clearly that it is not he who *decides*, it is obvious that answering all their questions would take my time and energy away. Would it be a good time investment? **Absolutely not.**

Investing in the *right* customers means concentrating the energy on those who can bring us turnover. Engaging twenty minutes in conversation with a customer can be a wise move if this customer has one or more of one of the features that make him a target customer and therefore for us *interesting* (purchasing power, decision making power, predisposition listening, needs expressed or unexpressed in line with the proposed product).

Conversely it will be a waste of energy if I invest twenty minutes with all the customers I call, hoping to conclude a sale. Not only is it a way to quickly deplete enthusiasm and energy, but it is also a crude method that hopes only in the law of large numbers to succeed, firing in the heap with eyes closed hoping to hit the center. It is a method that I personally detest and that has caused so much trouble for the market. For the same reason I detest the expression "attempted sale", which I personally have never used, and that reminds me of Yoda's response to an objection by Luke Skywalker: «Don't try... Do!»

Does that mean you only have to talk to the *right* customers? Of course not. It means that the energy used for every single negotiation must be measured. If I think that a customer can be interesting and worth thinking about, investing my time and my energies will certainly do. If then the negotiation does not go as I hoped it doesn't matter, but I certainly did my job well. And paradoxically I could decide to invest energy even with a customer who apparently displays a lack of interest to my approach over the phone, because I am confident of being able to offer something interesting and to be successful with my arguments.

The judgement meter, then, on the *right* client is left to you, know only how to rationalize. Much of the rationalization of energy goes from a proper and structured method of work called **structured phone call** and that will be explained in detail in Chapter 7.

Chapter 3

Using the voice

In no training course regarding phone sales is it taught how to use the voice. However, we should all be careful of language in all its forms (even at the sound level) because, as we said above, the *how* we say things influence the final outcome of communication very much.

Towards the end of the years '60, Prof. Albert Mehrabian, a psychologist from the United States, conducted interesting research on the importance of different aspects of communication in bringing about a specific message. The result appeared shocking:

- Non-verbal communication (in particular related to body and facial mimics) has an influence of 55%;

- The paraverbal communication (tone, volume, rhythm of the voice, etc.) affects 38%;

- Words, the verbal content, count only for 7%.

Does that mean what I say doesn't count but just *how* I say it?

Absolutely not!

It means that the content is as important as the voice we use (tone, volume, rhythm), which affects, as we have read, 38%.

However, how many of us have invested time in their own voices? Has anyone ever participated in a training on voice that is not aimed at improving public speaking or diction?

Nobody studies to improve their own voice: don't you find it absurd? We invest a lot in our outward appearance when we work with the public, and when this contact takes place by phone we do not think at all to *beautify* our voice which is our main tool of work (let's remember, as we've seen above, that one of the three parameters that determine the success of the phone sale is the seller!)

Have you ever heard a song that you did not like, but then sung by another singer has excited you a lot? It is the most striking example of the fact that the voice makes a difference. In the case of singing, the voice is the fundamental driver for arousing emotions, as in public speaking the voice is the main driver to entertain the public and permeate it with emotions in such a way to retain the message that we want to convey.

Another topic that relates to the *attention curve* described in the previous chapter: how many speeches (lectures, lectures or even homilies) have you heard recently in which, after 10 minutes, your mind has not begun to ramble on the bills to be paid, the dental appointment and the phone call to the plumber completely losing focus on the current speech? Often because the interlocutor has a flat and monotonous tone of voice that induces distraction or sleep, even if the arguments they are talking about are extremely interesting. But to deal with interesting topics is not enough: to increase or keep alive the level of attention we must use also our tone of voice.

What about you? How many times do you hear your voice? And when you listen to it, don't you always feel that yours is a *bad* voice?

It is absolutely normal: it would be the same if you would look yourself in the mirror for the first time after several years. You would probably think you have a horrible appearance or simply not the one you imagined. Because we never listen to our voice, we find it *ugly* when we hear it. If in our opinion our voice is *ugly*, why should it be appreciated by our interlocutor?

We have now understood that the voice is a very important tool of work because it gives *value* to what we say, and certainly goes to add to our **toolbox** daily, together with the sales techniques and knowledge of the offer. However, as we said, no training course explains how to use and how to improve the voice.

One of the top Italian experts in voice training was the trainer and voice actor Ciro Imparato. Ciro Imparato made a science of the use of the voice, determining what he called and patented as the method FOURVOICECOLORS®.

In his book "Your voice can change your life", Imparato explores all areas of use of the voice, and creates a *pattern* of colours with which to identify (and consequently modulate) the different tones that we give to our voice. In particular, he creates a distinction between 6 types of voices: *positive*, coloured voices, and *negative* voices, devoid of colour.

In particular, it lists the types of *positive* voices divided between:

- ➤ YELLOW voice: It is the voice of liking, which we use, for example, when we meet someone and greet them, when we want to be witty, or tell a joke;
- ➤ GREEN Voice: It is the voice of trust, which we use when we share confidences with a friend, when we apologize, when we recount a dramatic moment in our lives, when we desperately want the person we are talking with to believe in us;
- ➤ BLUE Voice: It is the voice of authority, which we use when we exhibit a product/service, when we state a fact, or when we speak during an electoral rally;
- ➤ RED Voice: It is the voice of passion, which we use when expressing our feelings, when we proudly describe our creation, when we speak to others of the successes of our children, when we defend a friend wrongly accused.

Imparato in his book accurately recommends never to use the two *negative* entries:

> ➤ GREY Voice: It is the voice of apathy, an *extinguished* voice colourless, without verve. Imagine those university professors who hold one-hour lessons with a monotonous voice: after 10 minutes (see Chapter 2 on the attention curve) your mind is already wandering, thinking about your own business without following the thread of the discourse;
>
> ➤ **BLACK Voice**: The worst, the voice of anger, the screams to overhang the interlocutor, the voice of those who think that yelling is right.

Unfortunately, what often happens in the commercial calls that we receive every day is to hear predominantly the GREY voice, a voice without enthusiasm or passion. Now, if those who sell a product do not put passion to describe it, why should the person at the other end of the line buy it?

Needless to say that even the BLACK voice is completely detrimental to the morale of each interlocutor; When you scream you are always wrong, by definition. As Sergio Marchionne (CEO of FCA) said, «who screams is no longer right, has only more breath.»

When I met Ciro Imparato we talked for a long time about the conversation scripts that are used in the world of phone sales (see Chapter 7). He told me right away, «the FOURVOICECOLORS® method is my script.» Ciro meant that whatever we say, however interesting, must be accompanied by a proper voice. Would you ever say «I love you» to your partner with the same voice you order a pizza with?

So every topic that we exhibit must be accompanied by the right emphasis, and in particular in a *cold* commercial call:

- At the beginning of the call you will use the yellow voice (the liking): you must try to give right away (it is estimated that the first 5 seconds) the right impression to the customer. And to do that you have to use the voice, because the words, especially at the beginning of the conversation, are not immediately perceived by our interlocutor;

- Then you will switch to the green voice (the trust): trying to convince the potential customer at the other end of the phone that you are proposing something interesting and convenient for him/her;

- Then, you will use the blue voice (the authority) to describe with competence and authority the commercial offer that you thought of for your potential client;

- Finally, the red voice (the passion) will help you to give emphasis and passion when you answer their objections, to make them dream about the product with the eyes of the mind, to convince them that they are investing their money well.

Mastering these voices is a non-simple process that also requires the training support of professionals like Ciro Imparato. However, each of us can begin to exercise his own voice, to listen to it more and more often, and to try to vary it according to the times and the ways that require it. Fortunately, the use of WhatsApp and voice messages can help us for this point. Listening to your voice again and again after you send a voice message is strongly recommended in order to be able to self-evaluate and self-improve it. Once you have learned how to modulate your voice you will undoubtedly have a greater success in phone sales.

Paraphrasing a well-known sentence by Zach Holman **I am sure to say that a good voice will not make the product you sell magically desirable: but certainly a great product will lose all desirability if described with a bad voice.**

Chapter 4

The need

Now let's define the concept of *need*: what is it really? As described in the Treccani vocabulary, a need is «[...] any painful sensation arising from a present or anticipated dissatisfaction, accompanied by the knowledge of means to diminish, remove or avoid such suffering, and the desire to procure [...]»

Abraham Harold Maslow, American psychologist famous for his theory on the hierarchization of needs, helps us to understand the meaning of *need* from the psychological point of view. In psychology the need is "a state of tension due to the lack of something that responds to physiological needs (e.g. affection) or social needs acquired by the environment (e.g. success)". Maslow in 1954 proposed 5 basic needs, organizing them within a *pyramid* in a hierarchical way, from basic needs to those of higher level: physiological needs (survival), safety needs (protection), needs of affection (belonging, love), needs of esteem (personal consideration), needs of self-realization (realisation of its own potentialities and aspirations).

Without the satisfaction of the *fundamental* (or elementary, such as feeding, sleeping, protecting) needs, all other *superior* needs cannot be fulfilled. Translated into practice: if my first thought in the morning is to have enough food for myself, I will not lose time to carefully choose the dress to wear and I will certainly not write a poem.

In the world of sales this scheme becomes fundamental to understand the positioning of the product that is sold inside the pyramid. When you sell by phone, then, you always have to determine what customer need we are trying to meet and prepare all of our negotiation accordingly.

Let's show you an example: those who sell house alarm systems know that their product is positioned in the segment concerning safety, and then they will study all the promotional activities and communication aimed at gaining awareness of this need to the customer, since they already have the right tool to satisfy it. It is similar if I sell a self-defence spray: my task will be to persuade my interlocutors they need more security, and then a pepper spray is the right object to always carry with them.

In the famous film "The Wolf of Wall Street", Leonardo di Caprio aka Jordan Belfort, in a scene tests the sales capacities of his entourage asking everyone to be able to sell a pen. Only Brad succeeds in creating a need. But how do you create a need?

The need sometimes doesn't even have to be created because we all have needs that can be expressed, but also others that are unexpressed, latent needs that wait only for the right moment to be awakened.

The good salesman is able to transform unexpressed needs into expressed needs. Regarding this, it is of some help the story of the two shoe sellers sent to find a new branch in a village in Central Africa. As soon as they arrive, realizing immediately that all the inhabitants walk barefoot, the first salesman calls and reports desperate: «there is no market here for our product, all the inhabitants are barefooted. I'm going home. » The second instead calls in place and says enthusiastically: «Send me another load of shoes: market here is virgin; we can do great business! »

It is certainly much easier to sell a product that satisfies an expressed need: if you sell a phone subscription, you do not have to explain to the customer why it is useful to have a mobile phone and what great advantages they will have in owning one. On the contrary, if you sell a life insurance policy, you have to convince your clients, first of all, that it is wise to buy such a product, even before you can argue about the convenience of your product or make comparisons with your competitors. Clearly the sale in this case is much more complex, because you are proposing something that does not meet an explicit need of the customer, rather an implicit need (savings, security for the future, retirement, etc.).

Understanding the needs expressed, and intercepting the unexpressed needs of the customer, knowing how to read *between the lines* of what our interlocutor tells us, is one of the talents that every good seller must develop. In most cases (especially in outbound activities) the potential customer does not clearly express his needs, thus making it complicated for the salesman to understand on which levers to act to convince him that the product he is proposing fully satisfies his needs.

The main question that a seller must have in mind during a telephone conversation when the customer has objections is: «what is the real obstacle for the customer? Why he is not buying?».

We will talk extensively in chapter 7 about the management of objections.

Chapter 5

The cost-benefit balance

A cost-benefit balance is a decision-making mechanism that we all apply as customers when we buy something, and which we must always take into account when we are selling a product. Consider that each of us always has this balance in mind when making a purchase, evaluating what is called *value for money*.

Imagine the classic two-plate scales: one plate will represent the COST and the other the BENEFIT. Arm yourselves with small imaginary weights and put them one at a time in their respective plates.

The COST: it is a burden that is very clear in our head. We know exactly the worth of 10, 20 or 30 euros, and what sacrifice entails having to spend it. Let's place, then, our first small weight in the plate of the cost.

The BENEFIT: It's something we don't know about. We perceive it when we want to buy a product and we have to decide whether that product is worth the economic effort. Every single weighing is made up of an advantage that that product will give us by buying it.

At the moment that the seller proposes a product, therefore, the cost plate is already heavy: the benefits are at the moment empty, so the tilt of the scale is decidedly in disfavour. Remember that the customer will only buy if the tilt of the scales is in favour of the benefit plate. Otherwise he will never buy, no one likes to spend money foolishly!

How do we then put the weights in the benefit plate? Simple, from time to time adding all the benefits from buying that product. Then the customers will draw their deductions coming to two possible conclusions: buy (because they have understood that the product will give them benefits that are worth the price paid) or not buy, concluding that the product is too **expensive**.

Attention, remember that *expensive* does not mean «I do not like» or «I do not care.» It means that the benefits offered by the product/service are not judged sufficient for an economic sacrifice of that kind.

There are two methods to balance the plates:

> a) lighten the cost plate, for example, the shopkeeper who, in front of the customer hesitating on the purchase, decides to give him a small discount to break his resistance;
>
> b) increase the weight of the benefit plate.

Solution A is of course hardly feasible in everyday activity, without affecting the company's income statement. So you just have to learn to increase the weight of the benefits. But how do you do it?

Here the intervention of the seller (yours) is needed. In a cost-benefit assessment it is the seller who makes the difference: he/she stands next to the balance and helps to put more and more weights in the benefit plate. Because the seller knows the benefits of his product, having been appropriately trained on the subject, and his ability to transmit them effectively will be the reason for his success.

As we said in Chapter 2, selling means conveying the benefits and advantages of a product/service from you, the sellers, since you know them perfectly (thanks to your training) to the potential customer who, instead, does not know those benefits. The seller is the one who is the deputy to *tell* the benefits to the customer.

Let's show you an example: you enter a shop and see a shirt that you like, you pick it up and peek at the price tag (100 euros). You are going to put it down, thinking that it costs too much when the salesman arrives and cheerfully says to you: «Excellent choice! Do you know that this jersey is in mixed cashmere 100% made in Italy? The colour is awesome! Consider that the fabric is tested in order not to lose colour even after hundreds of washes. It has this price only because it is the last piece left, if you observe the tag, originally it cost twice as much.»

Would you buy? I don't know. Certainly without the contribution of the seller you would have put down the shirt and you would have left the store convinced that the shirt was too expensive. But now you are wondering that maybe you should not miss this opportunity, since it is at a discounted price! In any case, without the salesman you would never have known about these benefits that, in one way or another, will affect your decision. That is why the seller makes a difference. But to make a difference you have to be aware of all the facets of your product (strengths and weaknesses) and skilled in transmitting the concepts to the potential customer.

Underestimating the seller's function in managing the cost-benefit balance is a common mistake. Large retailers are an example. In hypermarkets, the placement of the weights in the two plates is left entirely to the customers who, left alone, decide whether a product is worth the expense, thereby tirelessly hunting the *promotions* and *offers*, since the price represents the first motivation to purchase. But also in other sales channels we see situations in which the vendor fails to function as a *balancer*. How many times have you ever asked a salesman or saleswoman: «Sorry I'm looking for a pair of jeans», and to hear the answer «Look, you find them all in the wall over there...? » Also in this case the customer is left alone drawing ideas on the convenience of what he wishes to buy.

Give value

Let's take the example of the shirt described before to elaborate another concept.

You have picked up the shirt and you have peeked at the tag with the price (100 euros). After careful consideration, you decide to buy it. You pay, get out of the store, and tell your friends that you're happy with the purchase, but you had hoped to spend a little less.

Now rewind the tape.

Suppose that the shirt doesn't have any tags. You approach the cash desk to ask the price. The cashier tells you he can't provide it, since there's no barcode, and he asks the colleague, who at that moment is on the other side of the store. The colleague, forced to scream to make himself heard, tells him that the shirt is one of the last remaining pieces of a stock, and since it has a special price, he suggests using one of the barcodes present in the crate near the reader. The cashier, confused, replies that he does not know which code to use, whereupon the colleague answers: «The one of 199 euros». The cashier passes the code, turns to you and tells you «Ok, the shirt is 99 euros, will you take it? ». Having realized that the cashier has misunderstood the price, you hurry to buy the shirt, and come out of the shop rubbing your hands and boasting to all your friends of the great deal that you obtained.

In both examples the shirt is the same and the purchase price is also the same. What has changed? In the second case you are more convinced that you have made a good purchase because you have given a value much higher than the object, compared to the first example in which, instead, you are convinced that you have paid neither more nor less its value.

The attribution of the value of an object is therefore flexible and can be affected by various factors. Cialdini in his book tells us about the universally accepted axiom expensive=good, a cliché that resists time and still conditions the purchases of millions of people.

Balance in your mind

At this point in the manual it should be very clear that my strong conviction is that each customer is different from the other. Being awareness of this makes us clear that selling is personal and that levers that determine success do not shrink to mere *price*, but there are other factors such as: time, *anxiety* to make a bad purchase, security, impacts on health, etc.

From this we draw an obvious conclusion: when you talk to a potential customer you have to always have in mind that you are not selling **the product/service** but you are selling the reason why they will use it.

This concept perfectly follows what I was initially talking about: the *personalized* sale. I can't think of proposing the same product in the same way to "n" people. I have to understand if the product can be appropriate to my interlocutor and in what way, and then explain to him why, in my opinion, the product is useful to him. I can sell a bottle of fine wine to a non-drinker if I explain what **he can do with it** (for example, give it away as a present, or keep it in order to earn a future value), certainly not without having understood what motivates the customer to buy it.

Chapter 6

Empathy

We usually wonder about *empathy* when we talk about sales. In all sales training courses, in fact, the word *empathy* is always present. It is always said that we must all have *empathy* with the customer, that we have to be *empathetic* during a sale (as if *being empathetic* is a Jedi mental technique to use during a treatment). But in all these cases there isn't an Obi-Wan Kenobi that explains concretely how to do it. So, what is really empathy and how can you be really empathic? We will try to understand it together.

Identifying ourselves with the customer: a common mistake

In my career, I've trained dozens of phone sellers. Once the headphones are worn, the most common mistake that I noticed in a new seller is not a technical error or procedural error, but a psychological error and that is the most common and most serious that you can make when you as the seller: identify yourself with the customer.

Harrison Ford loves to play the character of Indiana Jones. We all think that in that role he is very convincing. However, Indiana Jones hates snakes, while Harrison Ford not only appreciates them, but is also an expert on reptiles, skills he acquired when, as a young man, he was a Boy Scout. As Ford says, «the work of an actor is similar to that of a carpenter: you have to shape.» So, despite that, the actor can identify with the character to make it credible, at the same time it does not mean that in real life he will do what his character usually does!

The most common mistake that sellers often make is to identify themselves with the customer: thinking «I would never buy this product... Why should my client buy it?» This becomes evident when, during training to sellers who have to propose a new product, they begin to make a thousand objections to the difficulties they will encounter during the sales proposition, without even having first tested the market. These attitudes arise from personal considerations and prejudices that have nothing to do with customer feedback. The salesman always tends to offer what he likes best, what he knows best, what he knows can will appeal to the customer, often to the detriment of the company objectives.

I'll give you a tip: NEVER identify yourself with the customer because you are not your client. You probably don't act like him, you don't have his way of thinking, you would never buy the things he buys. Entering into *empathy* with the customer – as we said before, a seductive expression that is used in all sales courses - basically means aligning yourself with the mindset of the customer and being able to look in his direction. Together, seller and customer are thinking and evaluating things using the same criteria and the same yardstick, and relying on the same logical pillars.

After the axiom that it is dangerous to *identify* yourself with the customer, it must be clear that empathy, in the world of sales, cannot be the mental state of "put yourself in the shoes of the other". In my experience, I can say that success in sales increases proportionally to what we understand about our potential customer (not putting ourselves in his shoes!), and when we understand his needs and advantages derived from the uses that he will make of our product.

The key word, then, is **understanding**. We need to figure out who our interlocutor is so that we can develop an effective sales strategy. Paraphrasing a famous phrase from Sun Tzu's "Art of War", we can say that «If you know the customer and yourself, your victory is safe. If you know yourself but not the customer, your odds of winning and losing are the same. If you do not know the customer and not even yourself, you will succumb in every battle. »

Always in his famous book, Sun Tzu explains the importance of having information before facing any battle. And this is another key point: having information about the person we are calling will help us get to know it better and devise an approach strategy that is convincing. On the other hand, Sherlock Holmes also says in the book "A study in scarlet": «It is a serious error to theorize before having certain data. We end up distorting the facts, to adapt them to theories, instead of adapting theories to facts. »

To better understand a customer, it becomes essential to study him before even calling (see Chapter 7). Once this data is absorbed, we must *frame* this customer, and understand which commercial leverage would be effective for him. As we have read before, we cannot think of using the same approach with all customers because in some cases our techniques would be ineffective, if not counterproductive.

In this regard, the **Whole-Brain model** of the famous psychologist Ned Herrmann comes to our aid. Author of the Whole-Brain Thinking Model™, Hermann metaphorically attributes four styles of thought to four regions of the brain. These four quadrants (A, B, C, D) can be characterized as: A = goals driven, B = results driven, C = people driven and D = vision driven. To these styles, Hermann attributes a colour:

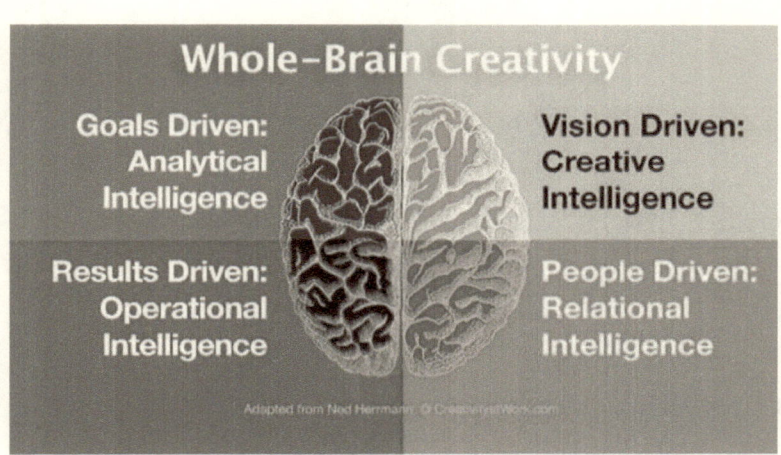

The idea is that the style of thinking of each one of us is composed of the sum of these 4 colours that, proportioned in a different way, determine our way of reasoning.

Through a special test, in fact, the Wholebrain™ method is able to determine each person's percentages about one component rather than another. It is unlikely to have 100% of a single colour, the most common configuration is that of a mix of colours where usually a colour (or a pair of colours) stands out on other styles of thought.

The four colours

A person with a more pronounced percentage of BLUE (logical) is a person who:

➢ argues rationally

➢ is logical

➢ is clear about the final result

➢ analyses critically

- is interested in facts, not theories
- evaluates carefully
- is rational, not emotional
- considers the economic factor
- is interested in goals and results
- is realistic, he keeps his feet on the ground

The person who, however, has a style of thought predominantly GREEN (organizational) is a person who:
- thinks that there is a place and a purpose for everything
- believes that «until it breaks, there is no need to fix it»
- is punctual
- has a practical approach to problems
- is consistent
- makes detailed plans and procedures
- does one thing at a time
- has an accurate compliance with protocols and procedures
- is disciplined and reliable
- loves order and control

But people with a greater percentage of RED (interpersonal) are people who:
- love people and group dynamics
- have empathy and education
- think that experience is the mother of wisdom

- are intuitive and comprehensive
- believe that values are important
- are participative and collaborative
- are expressive, long-winded, friendly
- are spiritual

Finally, the person who has high percentages of YELLOW (creative) as the primary colour is a person who:

- takes risks
- recognises new possibilities
- retouches or challenges institutional rules
- solves problems with intuition or instinct
- uses metaphors
- is original
- uses imagination
- is curious and adventurous
- has an artistic vein
- loves variety and multi-tasking
- imagines the future

But how do we recognize a style of thinking? Certainly through the attitudes and expressions of the people you want to have as your customers.

The above list already gives you an idea: for example, a BLUE customer will be interested in the function and purpose of the product you are selling, and less attentive to the small details, details that instead interest GREENS who want to know every tiny detail of the product they are buying. REDS will be more interested in the emotions and sensations that the product can arouse, often being guided by the purchase from the advice of friends rather than the product itself. And finally YELLOWS will be attracted by the uniqueness and originality of the product and the fact that, perhaps, it is a unique and original piece.

As a result, even your mental attitude will have to be in sync with the customer and adapt to his style of thinking.

- With a potential BLUE customer, we will talk about facts because he doesn't care about the *fluff*, and we will take care to be clear, brief and precise. We are going to do an objective analysis and argue in a straightforward, no-frills way.

- With a GREEN customer we will elaborate the details, like the contractual norms, the activation procedures, the technical parameters. We will give exhaustive explanations and will be careful not to ever go off topic.

- With a RED customer we will underline the value of the customer-seller relationship, we will be open and sincere, we will quote real life stories and we will argue with concrete examples.

- With a YELLOW customer we will use many metaphors, we will give the whole picture, we will make him dream, we stimulate it to change (which he/she loves).

In practice

From theory let's go to practice: suppose that you want to sell a smartphone to a potential customer. Listening to his needs and deducing his style of thought from the questions he asks, you will understand his personality and leverage certain arguments:

If the customer has a predominantly BLUE style of thinking he/she:

> ➢ will want to know how long the battery lasts
>
> ➢ will compare other smartphone models with the one he/she wants to buy
>
> ➢ will assess the cost of the accessories

- will be interested in performance in terms of power and speed of connection
- will have done research before buying so he knows exactly what he/she wants

If the customer has a predominantly GREEN style of thinking he/she:

- will be interested in the reliability and duration of the time
- will ask questions about the resistance of the apparatus
- will ask about the maximum standby time during the day, how many GB of storage, how many photos can be stored before running out of space, how large is the display screen
- will be interested in accessories, power banks, cloud backup of your phone
- will need to understand every single detail about how it works

If the customer has a predominantly RED style of thinking he/she:

- will evaluate the purchase from the first impression: from the handiness of the smartphone, to the comfort of taking it with him
- wants to *fall in love* with the product
- will love the simplicity of the functions
- will be sensitive to the receptivity of the seller and also take into account the after-sales assistance
- will go more by instinct than rationality in the choice of the product
- will take into account the opinions and advice of relatives and friends before purchasing the product.

If the customer has a predominantly YELLOW style of thinking he/she:

- ➤ will above all take into account the aesthetics, the colour, the originality
- ➤ will want to buy his dream phone, will not be happy with a second choice product
- ➤ will love to experience
- ➤ will buy the latest model
- ➤ will take risks investing in the purchase of new things

As described, the above is just an example of what you can expect from your interlocutor and consequently what will be the issues that, during the negotiation, we will tend to deal with and emphasize.

Once again I reiterate how important it is to know your interlocutor to be able to conclude a sale: we can succeed in a negotiation by giving to the customer exactly what he is looking for, and satisfying his perplexities on the more delicate topics. The Wholebrain™ model is a very effective method (for more info you can consult the institutional site) but there are also other models for understanding the psychology of the client.

As already mentioned in the past chapters, it is a mistake to think that you can set a business negotiation in the same way regardless of who is the interlocutor, or to think that a low price is the main lever for any customers.

Chapter 7

The structured call

Like many other activities, even to be able to sell on the phone you need to be trained in the methods and techniques to use. In my career I have witnessed dozens of preparatory courses at the beginning of the activity of future telephone sellers and I have rarely seen courses well done or well structured. Very often, training courses are a summary of the commercial offer, and they simply explain to the candidate what to sell, giving basic notions of communication (often difficult to apply over the phone) or a kind of vademecum on how to respond to the most common objections.

While for many jobs there are methods and procedures that are taught to the candidate, in the world of telephone sales I have never seen a structured method applied to the phone call if not based on empirical considerations given by those who know this job very well and would like to transmit sales techniques to the others.

To bridge this gap, we will now introduce the method that should be used for every sales call. This method, which I personally use from 2001 and with which I have trained dozens and dozens of phone sellers, is called the **structured phone call method**. This method is nothing more than a *modus operandi* that you should use to set up a sales-oriented call.

It is a big mistake to think you can improvise when making a commercial call: you cannot make a sale if you are not adequately prepared A) on the product to sell and B) on the methodologies used to sell.

BE PREPARED

The preparation is therefore fundamental, and I am not only talking about classroom training on the product. It is necessary to have a good dose of curiosity about the product itself, self-training even after working hours, showing interest in topics that can be related to the product you are selling. Self-training, in particular, must always be constant: exploring the competition, staying informed, reading all the news about what the market offers, are all actions that help to be constantly prepared and competent, and consequently have more success in the telephone negotiation.

Competence makes us credible interlocutors for the customer on the phone and the credibility of the seller is all in this business. No one likes to buy (then entrust their money) to sellers scarcely competent no matter what they are proposing.

Before you start calling, practice improving your voice (as described in Chapter 4). Remember that the **first goal** of a commercial call is to establish a dialogue with your customer/prospect. Only **after** having established a fruitful dialogue we can think of reasoning about commercial proposals and everything that follows. Be captivating and fascinating and you will be more successful.

THE SCRIPT

The conversation script, as you know, is universally adopted (and in many cases mandatory) in all departments that deal with the telesale of a particular product. In its original purpose, it should contain a series of carefully chosen sentences containing absolutely positive messages and expressions of *pampering* towards the client. The script is the same for everyone and is given to all the sellers in order to understand how to approach the customer and carry out the call.

Personally **I hate scripts**. I think they are the depersonalization of the phone conversation. Because they are the same for everyone, they create a terrible *copy and paste* effect that makes me nauseous. As we said, the phone conversation is pure creativity and can never be the same, or handled the same way for "n" times. The most appreciable aspect about this job is its variety, the possibility of dealing with dozens of different people every day, who, since they are all different, make every reaction unpredictable and any interaction different from the previous. And we want to copy and paste the conversation process by giving all the sellers an identical speech for everyone? It's sheer madness.

If we make the **same** call to hundreds of people, they will perceive it. Someone might argue that it's true that a phone salesman makes dozens of calls in a day.

It is true. But the secret is not to make people perceive it: nobody likes to feel *one of the heap*, and that's why the secret of this craft is to personalize (I will be never tired of saying it) the call according to the interlocutor who is at the other end.

On the other hand, people are different from each other, and also our phone call must be different, according to our interlocutor. Does anyone remember the modeling paste we used when we were children? Its advantage was the extreme modularity and simplicity of use. It could be put in molds to create funny objects, thanks to its high adaptability. Do you want to be successful in phone sales? Be adaptable!

As Darwin said, «It is not the strongest of the species that survives but the most adaptable.»

IDENTIFY THE DECISION MAKER

Whatever the name you have in your database, whether you are calling a private customer or a business customer, you must identify the Decision Maker. The Decision Maker is the one who has the decision-making power to accept or reject our proposal.

By default, the DM is the person who has the purchasing power and authority to buy our product. Within a family, for example, the decision-making power belongs to the couple, husband and wife, while in a company it is usually the CEO or the owner who has this authority.

Decision-making power, however, can be delegated. Especially in the case of companies of a certain size, it is obvious that it will not be the CEO to take care of purchases in person. However, it is obvious that he will have to *sign in* writing or verbally, any contract. So you can conduct a negotiation with another manager (for example Facility Manager), but you have to be sure that the authorised signing person is aware of negotiation, because he/she will have to give his/her final consent. If not, you will have to explain everything again to the authorised person, who, at that point, might reconsider and decide not to buy!

Unfortunately, the person who will answer to the phone will not be the one with whom you want to speak, nor, in certain cases, will he be inclined to allow you to speak to the Decision Maker. He or she is what I define as the *filter*: here are the tips on how to manage this person effectively.

MANAGE THE FILTER

I call it a *filter* because he/she stands between us and the person you want to talk to, often presenting barriers, and preventing you from talking to your Decision Maker, answering right away and without consultation: «Look, we are not interested».

But, as you know, only Decision Makers can tell you «I do not care», and only from them will you accept a rejection. You cannot accept a rejection from a person deprived of the any decision-making power! So, how would you react?

You have to be extremely kind to the filter, and very gently let him know that you still want to talk to the the Decision Maker. In addition, you must try to get all the information that can be useful to you for future negotiations. For example, suppose you call a company saying: «Good morning, my name is Andrea and I work for Webfantastic, I would like to speak to the CEO, please.»

The person who answers, probably from the reception or one of the other offices, will answer that the CEO is busy, and he/she will suggest you call later (typical!). At this point the classic telephone seller, greets and thanks, planning another call the next day.

Absolutely Not!

The person who responds to us, however is not a Decision Maker. You may get information that may be useful for your future negotiation. For example: «Thank you, I'll call back at the time you indicated. In the meantime, may I ask you, if you know, what internet package has your company subscribed to? » or «Thank you, I'm trying to better know your company, because it's the first time I am calling. If I can ask, how many employees work in your company? » or again: «Because I'm sure the CEO is a busy person, could you suggest a time when he is less busy? »

So, you must always understand what information the filter is able to give us because he helps the lead profiling, giving us his (sometimes long time) knowledge of the company.

You could discover, for example, that the company you are calling produces unique articles exported all over the world, and that it is at the forefront of a production sector. This information may be useful. So be nice to the filter and establish a friendly relationship, since he/she could give you a lot of support in the deal.

He represents a very important support that can, for example, help you to complete the company framework if you have out of date information in your database. Probably the CEO has changed, or you do not have the name of the new Facility Manager of that organization. In this case, the filter could help you a lot, because I can get in my very first call the name I wish to know. And, in my next call I will begin revise my approach in this way: «Good morning I'm Andrea and I work for Webfantastic, I would like to speak to Mr. White, please.»

Have you noticed that now the sentence sounds more *safe*? It is a straight request to speak with a very precise person and does not sound more like the classic *commercial c*all.

Let's remember that a better lead profiling will help us a lot in the negotiation. We can start from concrete information that we have acquired from the database but above all from the filter, and use this information in order to be able to better understand your customer once you are speaking with him (see Chapter 6). But if the filter refuses not only to put the call through to the manager you are looking for, but even to reveal his name?

Well, the secret is in **giving importance** to your call. If you are a professional salesman and highly motivated about the validity of the work you are doing, then you must be able to transmit the value of your call to your interlocutors. If they do not want to put your call through it is because:

- A) they are convinced that it is not important;
- B) they believe that they have the right judgment to assess whether or not it is important.

These are the two points you have to face. In the meantime, make it very clear to the filter that your call is **important** and that the information you can provide will be of interest to the recipient of the call. Then try to shake the filter's convictions can his/her judgement determine that your call is not really important and that, therefore, can be easily discarded without any doubt.

You will often hear from the filters «Sorry we are not interested.» Try to gently question this statement. Bet on the validity of what you are proposing by telling the person that you have no doubt that the recipient of your call will be interested in listening to you and that, in any case, you prefer to hear his opinion. Let's remember that the filter **is not** the Decision Maker and only the Decision Maker can classify your call as "not interesting". We will not accept a NO from anyone who is not a Decision Maker!

It might also happen that the filter could answer: «You can speak with me; I will report to him.» Remember to never make the mistake of describing the commercial proposal to the filter; you would only burn your negotiation because the filter, while reporting, would be neither convincing nor as clear as you, ending up frustrating your work without ever having talked to the Decision Maker. Otherwise, if the filter is your close ally and has all the interest that the Decision Maker purchase your service, you can ride the wave of his enthusiasm to let him prepare the ground for you when you will finally speak to the Decision Maker.

Remember always that yours is not the **usual** commercial call, yours is an **important** call.

«ARE YOU INTERESTED?»

Whoever has been in a typical souk in an Arab country knows well that going around through the stalls of the market you can see hundreds of interesting items, but you have to be very cautious about asking for the price. Asking the price of an article to the stall holder means that you are interested in buying it, so your question will start a fun (and sometimes exhausting) negotiation, where the seller will not let you go until you buy.

Mirroring this scene with a telephone negotiation, you understand that you will never ask the customer: «Are you interested?» or «We could talk about it if you were interested...» and again, «What do you think, it might be interesting for you?»

The answer, in 99% of cases, will certainly not be a «YES!» but, at the limit, a completely elusive response. A «YES» said by the customer would be binding (for the principle of consistency described in Chapter 2) with a commitment to buy the service. So the question is basically useless and in many cases counterproductive because it gives room to the customer to answer a dry «NO!» closing the doors to any relaunch in the negotiation.

The customer's interest must always be taken for granted. If, in fact, the customer had not the slightest interest in what we are telling him, rest assured that he would have blocked us long before or would have given us clear and unequivocal signs of intolerance to our arguments.

Every time I make this recommendation to phone sellers, I always tell the story of what happened to a friend of mine. This guy met a girl on holiday who he liked a lot and after several unsuccessful attempts finally managed to invite her into his room. While it seemed that things were taking the right turn, he, overrun by the embarrassment of the moment, said to her: «Well, we are going to do it?». Needless to say, the girl fled after he had completely destroyed the romantic atmosphere.

Never ask «are you interested? » as you never ask «we are going to do it? ». Just do it, don't ruin the atmosphere.

FEAR IN SAYING THE PRICE

The fear of mentioning a price to the customer, especially if it is high, arises often from identification with the customer itself (see Chapter 6). Many sellers hesitate to say the price especially when they believe (sometimes based on absolutely personal considerations and not proven by customer feedback) that will be interpreted in a negative way by the interlocutor.

As in all situations concerning the sale, you must always flaunt security, even and especially when you say the price. There are various schools of thought about when to communicate it to the client: some people say that the price should be said only at the end of the negotiation, there are those who communicate it immediately because they think that with the price (if low) can immediately capture the attention of the customer, starting from the (wrong) assumption that the price is **the only driver of sale**.

The truth is **that there's actually no rule about it.** During a commercial negotiation there are customers who ask you immediately «Yes, but how much does it cost? » because they suspect that the fantastic product you are proposing is exorbitant, and will not follow you during the rest of the conversation until you will clear this doubt. On the other hand, being reluctant to communicate the price makes the customer feel you have something to hide. It is also true that blaming immediately the price of the product you are proposing merely diminishes its value, making it pass for a weak product that is sold in bulk.

The price of the product can be communicated when you feel that the conversation is sufficiently mature to ensure that the customer is ready to transpose the cost: the *how* counts more than the *when*. It is essential that, when you communicate a price, you should immediately transmit all the benefits that derive from that price to the customer, according to the mechanism of the cost-benefit balance described in Chapter 5.

So never tell the customer «The subscription costs 29 euros per month: what do you think?» Rather you will communicate the cost by saying «The subscription has a price of 29 euros per month and includes: unlimited access to the gym, four lessons of Zumba Fitness, and free use of the heated swimming pool.»

Always remember the axiom seen earlier: the sale is not *sell* something to someone, but the ability to transmit the benefits of a product or service from the issuer (the seller) who knows them perfectly, to the receiver (the customer) who does not know them or does not perceive them.

THE METHOD IN DETAILS

Let's get to the point: what is a **structured phone call**? It is a method that must be used to make a commercial call. Like all working instruments, this instrument must also help us to be more efficient.

Now let me ask you a question: who do you think performs, the seller who makes 100 calls and gets a sale or the salesman who makes 10 calls and gets a sale?

Of course the second is the most performing. And for two reasons (the second is the less obvious):

> A) he spared leads: with less raw material available he managed to achieve his goal;
>
> b) he is less tired, thereby maximising his energies during his work shift.

This method, mainly, helps to optimize the work of the seller: as said, you have no need to make hundreds of calls per day, you can be successful with a few but well done calls. Those who make hundreds of phone calls often *burn* leads that, managed by another seller, would instead bring more sales. Moreover, they don't even optimize their energy (as we have described in detail in Chapter 2).

The method of **structured phone call** arises precisely from the necessity to equip the telephone sellers with a precise method. Even in the field of sales, a method must be provided, since those who sell on the phone rarely receive a specific training.

Without any method of work, a phone seller is doomed to bankruptcy. Having a structured method is the key to success. Imagine, for example, having to plant nails on a wall and the only tool you have are your hands. You will probably use an entire day to plant a single nail (assuming that you can!). The situation changes altogether if, instead, you have an instrument (a hammer for example). You will greatly optimize the time since the appropriate tool has allowed you to achieve your goal. The comparison, I hope effective, highlights that the same work, but done with the appropriate tools, has a much higher success rate.

The method that I will teach you and which is described below is articulated in 6 telephone phases, that must not be reversed, skipped, or ignored. Let's see the pattern of the call in detail.

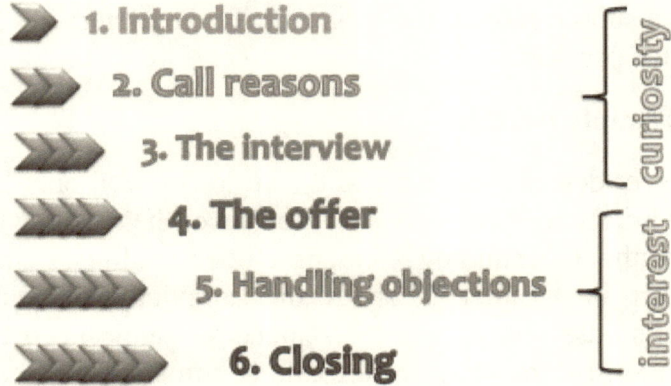

Step 1 – Introduction

This step in which you introduce yourself and your company. If the company is not well known on the market, it is necessary to add a brief description of the sector in which the company operates. For example: «Good morning, I'm Andrea and I'm calling on behalf of HerbalFresh, a company that produces natural cosmetics.»

Immediately after you have to ask to speak with the person or the owner of the company whose name you have in the form on your video, managing the filter with the techniques we have seen before.

About the form containing customer's data, take advantage of any information present to get an idea of the customer you are calling. If the data is very poor, try to qualify the lead, enriching the form with important details communicated by the *filter* (see paragraph about how to *manage the filter*). Therefore, if you need to call back, you will already have some useful data that will allow you to manage with much more ease the next call compared to a *cold* call.

Step 2 – Call reasons

Once we have the Decision Maker on the line with whom we want to talk, remember to avoid the most common mistake for the phone sellers: saying immediately at this phase the proposal you want to make to your customer. How many times are we called and we hear «Good morning Mr. White I'm calling to offer you a subscription to the magazine TopBigBeng with a great offer, only 22.90 euros per year...»

This approach is simply terrible!

In Phase 2 you never describe the offer to the customer: you only have to briefly explain (and briefly means a very short sentence) the reason why you are calling him/her, without mentioning prices, promotion or offers. Remember what I have written in Chapter 2 about the simplicity of telephone communication: let's use only simple sentences (subject, predicate, complement) to tell the customer why you are calling him.

Professor Robert Cialdini in his book "Influence: Science and Practice" talks about the power of the **because**. He describes the experiment performed by Dr. Ellen Langer who explored the principle that if we ask someone for a favour, we will have a better chance of being answered if we provide an explanation. The experiment showed that the simple request to use a photocopier could, if modified, have different outcomes. In one case the psychologist asked the people in line for the photocopier if she could skip the line and make photocopies before the others. In this case only 60% of the students agreed to this favour. But when in the phrase «excuse me, can I use the copier? » Dr. Langer added «because I'm in a hurry» 94% of the students let her to skip the line. The paradoxical element is that if the psychologist gave another reason, even irrelevant, the word *why* was enough to make her pass.

How does this translate into our work? If I say to a customer «I need to speak with you for a few minutes *because* I would like to share with you an important information» the customer will be psychologically more inclined to listen to you and to give you a few minutes of his time so you can explain your proposal.

Step 3 – The interview

At this point you connect logically from the previous phase and you ask a few questions to the customer to know him better and understand what kind of person he/she is.

This phase is fundamental because it is mainly useful as an icebreaker in order to better interact with the customer, letting him talk about himself, his passions, what he wants and how he wants it.

So you must always explain to the customer the reason for your questions and address them in the right way. The questions must be:

A) *Few*: the customer must not be subjected to questioning

B) *Pertinent*: closely linked to the purpose we are aiming for, do not ask futile things

C) *Motivated*: always explain the reasons for the questions

This phase is fundamental for another reason: the customer's answers will be the basis from which we start the negotiation. Do you remember the principle of consistency described by Cialdini? Human beings tend to be consistent with what they say.

The questions have precisely this aim: to make sure of the consumer's habits and to establish solid foundations. The customer who tells us that «he loves to go camping», cannot deny after a few minutes that he is a fan of outdoor activities; so if you are proposing the purchase trekking shoes we will depart from his previous statements to propose our product.

Regarding this, you must be very careful to undefined quantitative adjectives (little, much, quite, a lot, much, too much) because they are *undefined*. If a customer says «I watch TV for a little time» he is using a subjective measuring meter that could mislead. I could understand that the customer watches TV for less than an hour a day (according to me), when he is perhaps communicating to me that he spends three or four hours a day watching TV. This number of hours can be considered by him *a little time* according to his personal judgement. In this case you must always quantify the data with parameters that are universal and understandable by all without interpretations (for example the exact quantity). In the first example, I'll ask «For how long do you watch TV, more or less than an hour a day? »

Another tip is this: when the customer answers the questions, you have to always repeat what the customer has just told you: «So you're telling me that you just bought a new smartphone? ». This process increases the chances of happily concluding the negotiation, as Robert Cialdini tells in his book "Yes! 50 Secrets From the Science of Persuasion". A research by the psychologist Rick Van Bareen showed that the waiters of a restaurant who not only write in their notebook the orders, but they repeated word for word the order to the customer, obtaining almost 70% of tips more than before! This *mirror behaviour* as it is defined, has been the subject of study by researcher William Maddux who studied it applied to bargaining, demonstrating that *mirror behaviour* exponentially increases the confidence of the interlocutor and creates a favourable situation on both sides.

Obviously in the telephone sale the mirror behaviour cannot be applied to posture or gestures, but only relates to verbal expressions: so, as Professor Cialdini said, you can cultivate better relationships with customers by simply repeating their expressions, whether they are questions, complaints or orders.

Step 4 – The offer

At this point, being really clear about what the customer has communicated to us, you can elaborate your offer, suited to the customer's habits and personality and then find out the best way to propose it.

Usually, in a telephone sales activity you can have the opportunity to personalize the offer for the single customer, but it often happens that you have one or more standard offers that you must propose and that cannot be personalized.

If you work in a monoproduct environment, thereby proposing a single offer for all customers, you must comprehend (and in this case the interview becomes essential) what benefits of the offer can be suitable for that individual customer. So, in this case, your effort is not the customization of the offer, but try to understand how the benefits of your offer can coincide with those of the customer in a win-win negotiation.

Remember the Tetris, one of the first puzzle game born? How fascinating it was, thanks to its logic of interlocking: the challenge was to put all the pieces in their place. What you have to do is the same: to *trap* the benefits of your offer in the space of needs, expressed or not (see Chapter 4) of your customer.

If, on the other hand, you have the possibility to offer more commercial proposals, you will probably have a more complete (and therefore more expensive) and a less complete/expensive catalogue. Usually the cheapest offer is called *second choice* offer, because the company generally asks the seller to propose mainly a product or service and, if the customer finds it too expensive or unsuitable for his needs, bring to his attention another product with a lower performance and therefore less expensive.

What really happens? Very often the seller, fearing a «no» from the customer, or is hoping to make more sales, or simply making the mistake of identifying himself with the customer, proposes the cheapest product, which he judged more *easy to sell*. Unfortunately, in most cases, the telephone seller always points to the product easier to sell ignoring the one which is his duty to propose.

The fact that this way of thinking is wrong is not only a matter of opinion, but the result of an accurate study by Professor Cialdini, who describes this phenomenon in his book "Influence: Science and Practice" known as the principle of *perceptual contrast*.

Cialdini tells how real estate agents in the USA like to use this principle, showing the customer who intends to buy a house, some properties at an exorbitant price before showing him the house that they actually intend to sell.

As Cialdini tells us, the real estate agent said: «The house I had thought for them looked fantastic after having taken a look at a couple of slums.» A similar experience recounts a vendor of insurance coverage on audio/video products. This salesman had the task of proposing to the customer who had purchased a TV or a stereo an insurance cover of the variable service contract, from twelve months to three years. But three years were judged long time, so when he understood that the customer would never buy the 3-year cover, he proposed it first. When the customer rejected it, he proposed the twelve-month coverage that was accepted in 70% of cases, instead of 40%, which was the average of the insurance sales of that type in the store. And, incredibly, customers were fully satisfied of their purchase!

The *perceptual contrast* works like this: if you propose something more onerous, the second proposal, less expensive, will more likely be accepted than proposing the *economic version* as the first choice. It is a good mechanism that no seller must forget.

Now we can describe our offer in detail never forgetting the rules of telephone communication described in Chapter 1. We defend our product by also making comparisons with other competitors, if necessary, remembering a golden rule: never diminish the product of other competitors.

First of all because it is not professional: you have to propose your product because it is excellent, not because the alternatives are bad, otherwise it would lower the value of your product. Moreover, if your interlocutor is a customer of a competitor destroying the credibility of the competitor's product (which he currently owns) will do nothing but to put him on the defensive: as a matter of consistency, each person tends to defend the actions he/she accomplishes and hence the acquisitions he/she makes.

Have you ever bought something that you were not fully convinced about? All the way back home, you don't do anything but brood and question the goodness of your purchase. And when you have almost decided to bring it back immediately to the store to change your article, you arrive home and one of your family members see the product you bought and immediately begins to criticize it: how would you react?

In most cases, you will strongly defend your purchase and your choices, beginning to list all the merits of that product, even if you know, within you, that those criticisms make sense. Probably for pride or for consistency, you will keep the product, even if you know that you have not made a good purchase.

Do not put the client on the defensive: you have to stay on his wavelength, and not discuss his choices!

Step 5 - Handling objections

The management of objections is the stage in which we measure the skill of the seller.

Knowing perfectly well the product or service to sell is, as we said, fundamental. It is obvious, however, that you can never be ready for any objections that the customer may make, especially if you have recently started selling a certain product.

In this case the maturity of the seller comes into play; he must take inspiration from the customer's objections to learn even more about the product sold and be able to respond more effectively to future objections. Even a «NO!», in fact, is useful to grow and learn!

The person who has been selling the same product for a long time will clearly be much more skillful to answer the objections, but this is not always true. A skilled and expert salesman, studying the product, can immediately identify strengths and weaknesses and asks himself questions which in a negotiation could put him in trouble. In this case the seller tries to better understand the answers to the most common objections, before his customer could ask the same questions. But it could also happen that you receive some objections that have never been placed before, and therefore in this case you have to be always professional consulting those people who are competent and giving the correct answer. Whoever invents false answers when faced with an objection to which he does not know the answer, not only gives proof of lack of professionalism but also destroys his credibility in the eyes of the customer. Perhaps he might even be able to convince the customer, but as soon as the customer discovers the truth, he will despise the people who have deceived him and, of course, their company, which will suffer a huge image damage.

Always be professional and admit, when it happens, that you do not have the answer to the customer's question, reassuring him that you will immediately obtain the information that he asked. Obviously, if you can't answer nine out of ten questions it means you are unprepared, and maybe you would have never put yourself on the phone!

This is what I mean when I say that the good salesman is tested in the management of objections; in this case you can see in a glaring manner his professionalism, his preparation, and his ability to overcome the obstacles (objections) that the customer will pose.

As Ben Affleck says in his well-known film "Boiler room": «And there is no such thing as a no sale call. A sale is made on every call you make. Either you sell the client some stock or he sells you a reason he can't. Either way a sale is made, the only question is who is gonna close? You or him? » As you know, customers are great sellers, and they often manage to convince salesmen of the *truth* of their objections, even succeeding in causing them a loss of confidence in the product they are selling.

Always remember that for each customer there is an obstacle that prevents him from buying your product; always try to locate it. It is not easy because there are many people who declare outright what they don't like about your product, but other interlocutors, instead, advance objections that *hide* the real obstacle. These are called *unexpressed* objections and are distinguished from those *expressed* because they are subtle and very difficult to identify. If a customer, for example, said «I don't want to change my supplier», it could actually mean something else: he doesn't want to change because he's afraid of change. We all know that humans are resistant to change and probably have fear of the unknown, uncertainty or *unknown* frightens many people. So the real motivation for non-change could be a fear of modifying a status quo with which the customer is familiar, the anxiety to try new things, or the unpleasant idea of having to change his habits of consumption.

But rejection could also conceal other unexpressed motivation. The customer may not want to change because, for example, the seller has not given him enough motivations (benefits) for which he should do, or because he fears that his family would not approve a change in their homelife and they would criticize him for this, or even because he has the fear that the proposal, apparently very convenient, would truly be a halter contract from which will be very difficult to free.

As you see the same phrase can hide many meanings.

The main error that you can do when you receive an objection of this kind is to continue to exalt the convenience of what you are offering without dwelling to analyse the affirmations of the customer and investigate the real motives behind his refusal.

Basically it's like you're on a small road in Russia, and you see a sign in cyrillic. You do not know cyrillic yet you assume that it means "highway", while it really means "precipice". Better to understand the real meaning of the signpost before proceeding, right?

Again, as in the interview phase, always remember to repeat what the customer says, if for example he says, «I do not have much free time to go to the gym», repeat «since you do not have much free time I would like to propose...» This is useful, as said, to increase the customer's *liking* towards us.

Remember that sometimes the objections of the customer are an important cue to propose the most suitable product. Whoever, as in the above example, claims to have little free time we can answer: «So, you have little free time... a common problem nowadays! This is why we have our *open* subscription catalogue to make the most of the little free time we have, to keep us moving and improving our health!»

An interesting technique that can be used to overcome the objections of the customer on a given product or service, is the one that Professor Cialdini calls *the labelling technique*. This technique is well described in the book "Yes! 50 Secrets From the Science of Persuasion" and consists, as the word itself says, in labelling a person with a characteristic, an attitude, or a belief.

If you are proposing a subscription to the stadium, after the preliminary questions (for example, if the customer usually goes to the stadium or follows the local club) we can tell the customer «I understand from what you are telling me that you are very keen on your team» or «I understand that you are a passionate fan» or still «I am sure you are one of our best fans».

If I am proposing a sporting article I will say: «I perceive from your words that you love sports very much» or even «I am glad to hear this, you are really a careful and scrupulous person.» The action of *labelling* the interlocutor serves to make him aware (and in some cases proud) of his characteristic, on which perhaps he had never even dwelt. In this way, the labelled person is more and more convinced that what you have told him is completely true and therefore acts and behaves accordingly.

For example, when a boy has to choose a high school, if his teacher says to him «I know that you are smart in mathematics», he/she is operating a labelling operation that maybe will lead the student to choose a high school rather than another, based on this awareness of which, perhaps, he had never reflected before or of what he was not conscious. The student will probably go home expressing his preference for a certain high school motivating his choice with friends and relatives arguing that «mathematics is his fore».

Step 6 - Closing

It may appear to be the simplest passage, instead it is the most delicate. It is the moment in which you have to move from arguing and answering objections to the conclusion of the sale.

You cannot wait for the customer to take the first step and say: «Ok, I accept.» First of all, because it rarely happens, and then because you must always have control the conversation (see paragraph about how to *maintain control*). If you do not manage this phase correctly, you may experience two problems:

A) You hesitate in closing the negotiation: the customer will take the opportunity to postpone the decision telling you he wants to think about it (which means: forget as soon as possible what you said).

B) You have too much haste to arrive at the conclusion of the negotiation: you will give the unpleasant feeling to the customer that you want to a «Yes!» at all costs and that your sole purpose is to close the sale regardless of his satisfaction.

The closing phase, therefore, must be handled delicately. Once you have responded to all objections, and perceived that the answers that you gave him have been convincing, you proceed to invite him to provide you with the necessary data to conclude the sale, aiming to emphasize decisively the simplicity of the purchasing procedures (and if necessary or required of the rethinking procedures) and the appropriateness of the article chosen.

Always be safe and decisive, but without being impetuous or impatient, the customer must assimilate the information and be guided by you to the purchase, so you have to hold his hand during the entire purchase procedure, and not to push it!

Before concluding the conversation, greet and thank, remember that it is always a good practice to **quickly** summarize to the customer what he has just bought and what will happen from that point on. These will be the last sentences of your conversation and the ones that will be in his mind during the following days. The customer must not be forced to call the customer service to be reminded what he has adhered to, but he must be clear about everything and, above all, must remain well impressed even after the end of the phone call.

CURIOSITY AND INTEREST

Now that we have described the pattern in detail, let's look at the graphics a moment: as you can see the phone call, as well as being divided into 6 phases, is also divided into two macro-areas: curiosity and interest. At the beginning of the call, in fact, the customer is curious: curious to know why you are calling him, curious to understand better if what you are proposing can be useful for him, curious to understand what you are telling him.

But when we come to the middle of the bidding phase and the customer is listening to us, or even asks questions, it means that you have at least a minimum interest on his part. It is clear that the customer would not have let you arrive at this point if he were totally disinterested. This means that you must work on his interest, however small it is, to build a negotiation. This is another reason why you will never ask the customer if he is interested: as it seems logical, the interest of the customer is already there and must be cultivated.

For those who do inbound activities, the mechanics are more or less the same. The customer who contacts for information about a product or a basic service has some kind of interest: even then, no one who does not have a minimum interest take the phone to call customer service and learn more about a product. Even in the case of an inbound phone call, therefore, although there is no need for the first steps of the call (the presentation and the reason for the call) the mechanics are the same, and the real desire or inclination of the customer to buy is only granted during the management of the objections.

KEEP CONTROL

Have you ever seen the movie "Jerry Maguire"? In this film Tom Cruise is Jerry Maguire, a sports prosecutor who, fired after having written a memo considered scandalous by his company, tries to bring with him his old clients. In a rush to take with him customers, he unfortunately chooses to contact Rod Tidwell, a strong-willed football player who drags him into an endless call during which Jerry assists dismayed at the gradual reduction of his calls in tail, until, now prey to despair, hangs up the phone knowing that he has lost the opportunity to call many other customers.

This funny scene reminds us that we always have to be in control the conversation. The customer will often attempt, with a few sentences or questions aimed at destabilising us and drag us into some inconclusive discussion that is only going to waste our time. Remember: always bring the conversation back to the phase where it should be; don't be led to places where you don't want to go. If the customer wander and tries to divert you from your scheme, try to bring him back gently to the logical thread you intended to follow. If not, you will lose yourself in long and unproductive conversation.

During the telephone conversation, you have indeed to constantly ask yourself: «What step of the phone call I am in?» Remember that, mentally, you should never lose track of the structured call scheme.

Chapter 8

Rules to make an appointment

Within the sales area of a company, there could be a team that mainly deals with making appointments for salesmen, who make daily visits to customers. The activity of making appointments is vital for foraging a sales network that must have *fuel* everyday in order to make sales.

Having a scheduled appointment fixed over the phone agent is definitely a big value for a salesman. But it must be really an *appointment* and not a bare *rendezvous* as sometimes happens. The difference between a rendezvous and an appointment is that, in the first case, the phone agent does not discuss any offer with the customer, just making an open appointment in a place or time suitable for the customer. In the second case, instead, the agent creates a real business opportunity for the salesman by having aroused curiosity and interest in his customer, planning a visit that will have all the premises to be productive. Here are the 8 gold rules to make a good appointment for a salesman.

Rule # 1

As we know, it is a *must* to do a cognitive interview on the habits and personality of the customer: it is very important to also prevent any objections. The information collected must be reported, in a written form, on the appointment card so the salesman will have as much data as possible about the customer; he can use this data to think about how to set up a sales approach even before the visit has taken place.

Rule # 2

During the conversation you should never transmit the feeling that the visit takes place because the salesman has nothing better to do; it is very important to specify that the visit is made specifically for the single customer. The agent, then, must transmit the *weight* of the responsibility: committing the customer to be present (at home or in the company) for the visit, he/she must feel morally bound to respect the commitment made over the phone. It is useful, in this case, to borrow the example described above on Cialdini's studies: we will not tell the customer, «please call me if you have a mishap so I will warn the salesman», but we will transform the sentence in a question: «Will you call if you have a mishap that forces you to cancel the appointment?», thus exploiting the principle of coherence.

Rule # 3

It must be clear to the customer that the visit will involve the possibility of a contractualization. Therefore, the customer must be aware that, assuming that the information provided by the salesman is is satisfactory for him, it must be possible to conclude a contract or a contract request which in most cases requires the presence of a well-defined person (owner of the contract) with the power of signing a contract. This rule is fundamental when the Decision Maker delegates its decision-making power, authorizing another person to purchase the product or service, but certainly he is not delegating its signature power. Therefore, the presence of the Decision Maker will always be necessary (even if he does not participate actively).

Rule # 4

Let the customer choose the time and place of the appointment (if possible in planning the agenda) because it is much more likely to be convenient for him: remember to always meet the needs of the customer. In any case, try not to grant the absolute punctuality of the salesman, give a range of time, (even 15 minutes) useful to prevent any unforeseen events, especially when there are several other appointments on the same day. Do not set an appointment «at 4.00PM» but «between 4:00PM and 4:15PM». Unless the customer expressly requests the utmost punctuality, in this case you will warn your colleague that it is not possible to have a delay. With these little tricks you will avoid the customer getting impatient or make feel that he is not being respected: remember that the lack of punctuality is always a lack of respect.

Rule # 5

Mark an alternative contact number of the customer (fixed or mobile), especially if the appointment will not take place where we are contacting the customer (home or office). The alternative number will be useful for the salesman in order to be able to contact directly if he has any difficulty in finding the address or should he have a delay (see rule 4), but above all it is important for the phone agent. As a matter of fact, it is always a good idea to confirm all appointments that occur 24 hours after being made. If more time passes, there is a possibility that the customer forgets the appointment or gives priority to other commitments, taking him away from the place of the appointment. Just make a quick call the day before to remind him of the commitment made.

Rule # 6

In case the customer has already been contacted a first time and has made an appointment and cancelled for some reason (because the customer had a problem and had to, or the salesman did not succeed in going to the appointment, etc.) be very careful in the process of reconfirmation. This is a very delicate moment in which the customer could take advantage of what happened and can avoid making another appointment, claiming not to be interested since he has changed his mind. In this case, try to re-establish the appointment by repeating the previous negotiation, and using the same commercial levers (benefits and advantages) that previously convinced him to give his consent to the appointment.

Rule # 7

Respond clearly to any doubt or confusion the customer may have on the appointment and give him the information he needs: but be careful not to give him *too much* information. The customer must be interested but at the same time curious to know more, otherwise if he already knows every little detail of your offer, he will draw the conclusions (wrong, probably) and without the advice of your salesman about the convenience of your proposal, *burning* an appointment before it starts. Make sure that your customer is curious and interested and you will increase your chances of success.

Rule # 8

Let's use, as often as possible, the customer's language code. Remember that the lack of understanding creates discomfort: so if you work on a regional basis and your customer often uses slang words, do not be afraid to follow him, always maintaining a professional conversation but also using slang phrases and expressions that he used first. Moreover, exploiting the persuasive principle of *liking* described in Chapter 7, it is good to always repeat the exact terms used by the customer during the negotiation.

Acknowledgments

I want to thank all the people (and they are many!) who with their teachings allowed me to accumulate the experience that led me to write this book.

I deeply believe that, in the sales world in particular, people make the difference. Most of my experience has been built just listening to the feedback of my associates, colleagues and managers.

The sales techniques we use every day are not described in a textbook, but are experienced in the field every day, and then written down.

I would like to pass on my experience through this book, with the hope that it will be useful for you.

www.ingramcontent.com/pod-product-compliance
Lightning Source LLC
Chambersburg PA
CBHW030018190526
45157CB00016B/3129